THIS BOOK BELONGS TO

....

....

Scrapbooking Creating Memories

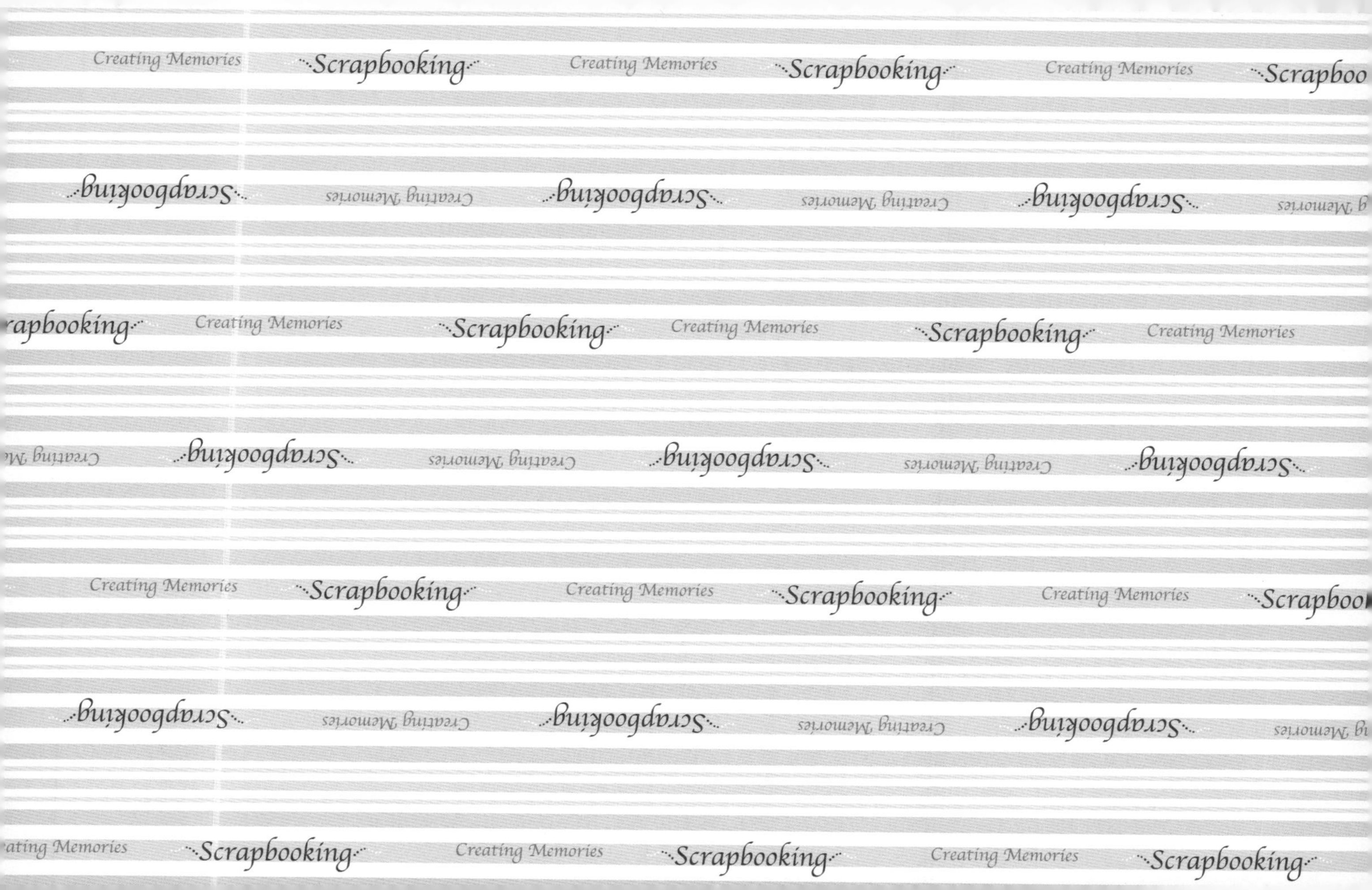
Scrapbooking
Creating Memories

Scrapbooking Creating Memories Scrapbooking Creating Memories Scrapbooking

Creating Memories Scrapbooking Creating Memories Scrapbooking Creating Memories Scrapbooking

Scrapbooking Creating Memories Scrapbooking Creating Memories Scrapbooking